MR HENDRIX
AND THE HALF EATEN MINCE PIE

© 2013 A.J. Foxx

All rights reserved. No part of this publication may be reproduced, stored in a retrieval system or transmitted, in any form or by any means, electronic, mechanical, photocopying or otherwise, without the prior permission of the publisher.

Hendrix the Pomeranian Puppy was soooooo excited.
He raced around the room getting very, very dizzy.
Round and round and round he went until…
He came to a sudden stop in front of an enormous Christmas Tree.
Tonight was CHRISTMAS EVE.

Hendrix sat in front of the Christmas tree and watched the fairy lights twinkling on and off, on and off.

"Oh 'endrix, it is so beautiful," purred Kitty the Toy Cat.

Kitty is French, she wore a diamante collar that sparkled in the fairy light.

"Ssssssssssssure is" hisses Sid the Snake. Kitty and Sid are Hendrix's best friends.

"Look at the glass baubles and the silver and gold garlands.

I helped Olivia to carry them," woofed Hendrix excitedly.

Olivia is Hendrix's owner. She had just gone out to pick some holly from the garden.

"There are so many colours," said Kitty.
"I can see blue ones, sliver ones, golden ones. Oh! Look, 'endrix, some striped red and blue ones too. They are all so pretty and shiny.
'Ow many are there 'endrix?"

Hendrix looked at the glass baubles.
"I can see 1…2…3……..blue ones," counted Hendrix.
"I can see 1……2…….stripy ones," gasped Kitty.
"Well I can see 1….2….3….4….5….ssssssssssix ssssilver ones," hissed Sid.
"You win!" woofed Hendrix, as they all flopped down on the floor.

Hendrix's nose crinkled up.

"What is the delicious smell?" he asked Kitty and Sid.

"I think Olivia is baking something in ze oven," said Kitty.

"Shall we go and look?" she said, running off into the kitchen.

"No!" barked Hendrix sternly.

"Olivia said I must never go near the oven or I might get burnt.

The oven is very, very hot!

Come back Kitty! Look at the fairy on top of the Christmas tree."

Kitty and Sid stared right up to the very top of the tree then they both gasped as they saw the elegant fairy.

" Oh 'endrix she is so beautiful. Look at her gorgeous, golden dress," sighed Kitty.
" And her sssssssssshiny fairy wand sparkles in the light," hissed Sid.
" Her wings, look at her golden wings!" woofed Hendrix gleefully.

At that moment Olivia came back with some holly. She went into the kitchen.
   "Stay back Hendrix I'm going to get the mince pies out of the oven and I don't want you to get burnt."

Hendrix crinkled his nose again as the delicious smell grew stronger.

"We must remember to leave one mince pie out for Father Christmas and a glass of milk, then we will save the rest for tomorrow."

Hendrix did not want to save the mince pies for tomorrow. He wanted one now! Olivia put the plate high up on the kitchen shelf and Hendrix could only sit and stare.

"Time for bed young man, we have to be fast asleep before Father Christmas gets here!" said Olivia.

Before he knew it Hendrix was fast asleep, with the smell of hot mince pies still in his nose.

Whoooooosh! .... Whoooooosh!
Hendrix sleepily opened his eyes.
Whoooooosh!................ Whoooooosh!............... Whoooooosh!

"What is that strange noise?" Hendrix asked himself.
His eyes widened in surprise. The fairy from the top of the Christmas tree was flying around the room.

It was the sound of her wings beating that had woken Hendrix.
She waved to Hendrix with her fairy wand then flew back to the Christmas tree landing daintily on the very top branch.

Hendrix rubbed his eyes,
"Did I really see the fairy flying?" he woofed out loud.
" Yes you did 'endrix," whispered Kitty.
" She ...."

But Hendrix's nose began to twitch.
He looked to the left,
he looked to the right and on a small table near the fireplace Hendrix saw a glass of milk and next to it a ......

MINCE PIE !!!!!!!!!
Quietly he tiptoed over to the table and sniffed the mince pie. Then quick as a flash his teeth bit into it and half of it was gone.
 "Sssssssstop," hissed Sid.
 "No 'endrix that is for Father Christmas," shrieked Kitty.
Suddenly there was a loud thump on the roof and as if by magic (which of course it was) Father Christmas was standing by the small table.

"Hendrix, what have you done? That was MY MINCE PIE," boomed Father Christmas.
Hendrix gulped. He looked up and up and up into a rosy cheeked face framed by a white curly beard.
Father Christmas put his hands on his hips and began to laugh.
"Ho .... Ho .....Ho...."
His whole body began to shake and he laughed and laughed until the tears rolled down his rosy red cheeks.
"Oh Hendrix, I'm only joking. I don't mind you eating half my mince pie. But tell me, is it a good mince pie?"
Hendrix nodded his head. He looked into the twinkling blue eyes of Father Christmas.
" Yes," he woofed. "It is the best half a mince pie I have ever eaten."

MR HENDRIX

Help Mr Hendrix find his way through the maze to Father Christmas

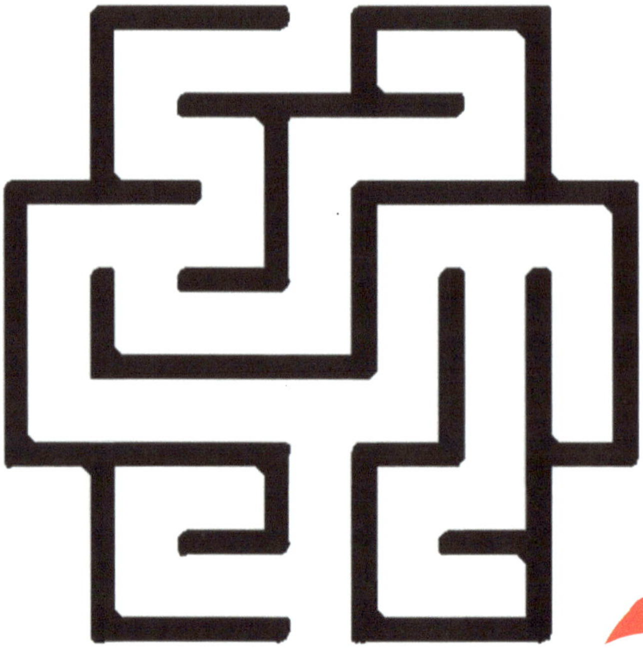

Can you help Mr Hendrix and Kity count all the presents?

MR HENDRIX

Can you colour in this picture for Mr Hendrix?

MR HENDRIX

Can you colour in this picture for Mr Hendrix?

www.ingramcontent.com/pod-product-compliance
Lightning Source LLC
Chambersburg PA
CBHW041234040426
42444CB00002B/154